CAPE POETRY PAPERBACKS

JEREMY REED
NERO

NERO

Jeremy Reed

JONATHAN CAPE
THIRTY-TWO BEDFORD SQUARE LONDON

First published 1985
Copyright © 1985 by Jeremy Reed

Jonathan Cape Ltd, 32 Bedford Square, London WC1B 3EL

British Library Cataloguing in Publication Data

Reed, Jeremy
Nero.
I. Title
821'.914   PR6068.E/

ISBN 0-224-02346-2

Some of the poems in this collection
have previously appeared in the follow-
ing sources: *Aquarius*, 'Migration';
Field, 'Daddylonglegs'; *Literary Review*,
'Heirloom'; *Poetry Canada Review*, 'Black-
berrying', 'Momentum', 'September
Cycle'; *Poetry Review*, 'Wounded Gull',
'Rabbits'; *Temenos*, 'Dead Weasels',
'Violets'; *Twofold*, 'The Music of Blue';
Two Plus Two, 'Bass'; *Verse*, 'Cornering',
'Apprehension'.

Typeset by Computape (Pickering) Ltd, North Yorkshire
Printed in Great Britain by Ebenezer Baylis & Son Ltd
The Trinity Press, Worcester and London

*In memory of Senta
and to Fred and Corinna*

Contents

I

II

III

IV

V

VI

I

Spider Fire

The popping crackle of dry sticks, the hiss
of catching gorse and broom, had routed out
all small things from the undergrowth, fieldmouse
and shrew, the glinting tick of the grass-snake,
squirrel and weasel, touchpaper-rabbits,
the conflagration spreading, red and blue
quiverings of flame quick to overtake
the fire's orange centre, timothy grass
and thistle sucked into the twitching crack
of the irregularly sheeting wave,
birds had gone in advance of the smoke plume,
rooks heckling in their flapping sky traffic,
chased off by a shuffling necklace of stones,
marigold, scarlet, crazy yellow whirrs
jumping a cow-gate, scorching the farm track . . .

What was the fire's shock through a spider's eyes?
The agelena's horizontal web,
pegged to a blackthorn hedge, scintillating
with rainbow filaments, male and female
telephonic in their alarm signals,
the vibrant nerves unleashed from a tight ball,
acrobats dropped down to the maze-forest
of verticals, a field away the roar
gaining in volume, everywhere a migratory
diaspora of insects, tunnelling,
feeling forward with bristling antennae,
the tenacious marauding wolf-spider
running across hairline fissures, halting
like someone pulled up short by a mirror;
some missing legs, armour-plate or an eye,

embattled hunters chased out of the field
by a seismic explosion, shivering
in the long drag of smoke, their collective
panic inducing a telepathy,
a radar bleep signalling the way out.

I watched from the hill's summit; a black hoop
ironed into the shire was a ring of ash
incinerating insects in its char.
The farm was black struts, ember-glowing spars.
Some must have made it to the other side,
two spiders having crossed a continent,
digging in, letting the earth still, aware
they'd made it, smoke-blind, too tired to hide.

Wounded Gull

Wind shifts the earth's face: grit and topsoil run
ticking through crevices, a migration
of tiny particles hissing inland;
wind blinds the red eyes of rabbits with sand,
gulls huddle inshore snowing down on farms,
already the Atlantic's beached a score,
a poulterer's accident, vertebrae
and necks smashed, plump bodies fouled by oil,
they're sucked back and thrown out by each wave's roar,
its dynamited blasting across flats.
What the sea ejects is misshapen, flogged
into the bare components of itself,

slatted, forcibly pitched into debris,
roiled back and forth, scoured pristine by the salt.
I came across dunes, intermittently
dropping into a hollow for shelter,
the wind pressing my brain back to a charge
that flickered like a light in a tunnel,
a fish forcing the opposing current,
and came down to the beach; flooding runnels
kept draining into the torrential surf.
I stood as a bird does facing the wind,
my toe stubbing the petrified shiver
of a gull dislodged from its bone structure,
the collapsed wings trailing, the bloody skull
showing the underside of its fracture.
I could have kneaded it into a ball,
and lobbed it back into the sea's mouth,
its twitching seconds of life dependent
on what few nerves still remained unsevered.
I took it back with me to the seawall,
and buried it, that too no permanent
act of consignment, but something the wave
or wind would upturn, and shake from its bones.
Tomorrow the flood tide would find its grave.

Dead Weasels

I found them hanging, strung up on grey cord,
five of them, gagged together with jackdaws,
the branch weighted like a poulterer's hook
with carrion worn through to their skeletons,
the walnut-sized ivory skull of a rook
had come loose of its rain-moulded bark-stiff
feathers, flushed on dead leaves no fox would sniff.
Dead silence, the wood stark, old beech, old elms,
defiantly rooted against the cold,
and, at the field's edge, rabbit diggings, flint
thrown up on the furrow. The light was gold
on plum-stained brambles. Somewhere else a gun
was barking sporadically at pheasants.
I swung the weasels round to catch the sun,
their long, slender bodies hung vertical,
the fur a straggling ripple on the bone
was like a current chased out in a stream,
the forepaws stylized, were two brittle hands
raised in supplication. The vice-locked head
seemed more a conger's raised to fight the gaff,
the jaws open upon their needle teeth
as though frozen in the bloody second
of ripping into a mole or chicken,
fast night-hunters who companion the owl's
plummet at a leaf-tick. These had their skulls
protruding through an envelope of fur,
crisp to a dryness that the thumb could peel,
rain-beaten fossils gone to matted rope
stringily twined, they looked like effigies
of a demonic rite without the pins.
I cut two down and placed them in a sack,
victims who'd raked the copse for pheasants' eggs,

and sucked them dry. They still had fine whiskers,
minute spiders bunched in the eye sockets.
Their combined weight was less than a finger,
their volatility still composite
in their death agony. Rooks and ravens
were thronging back in droves. I came on out
and crossed the field, my presence scaring off
two short-fused rabbits bolting for their dens.

Foxes

The beech leaf drums upon the sycamore,
the wood's splashed umber and scarlet, twilight
brings with it the floating cry of an owl,
an acorn popping from a cup alights

upon the swishing flick of a fast stream.
Sometimes I've heard the yapping peacock scream
of a vixen, or bark of a dog-fox,
announce the night, the moon a frosting gleam,

the air resinous with woodsmoke, leaf-rot,
damp tree-rime, bank moss. Once in the blue cold
a fox stood mucking out my garbage bin,
hunger had made his bloody instincts bold.

He vanished, sensing me at the window,
a farmer shot him in the poultry run,
the chicken jerking, its head bitten off . . .
He nailed the brush up as a russet sun.

Dissimulation's the art of the fox,
swimming downstream to ducks, sharp nose beneath
a raft of weeds, or lying on its back
playfully kitten-rolling on the heath,

feigning uninterest in the rabbits
it will grip by the neck, and skin alive.
Foxes climb trees, quarter a pastured lamb,
wallow in a mud coat, and then arrive

to tyrannize a foal hysterically,
they'll bite their leg off to escape a trap.
I shiver in the dark, a rabbit screams,
somewhere a collie's barking lends a map

to sunken farms, a fox is on the prowl,
engendering panic, moving unseen
through bracken, already paralysing
the rooster's head a snap will take off clean.

Rabbits

Rabbits the buffish-grey of scorched stubble
were bobbing into hill-sprints as my foot
opened the valley's silence – tinder leaves
crackling to a dry dazzle – a mulched soot

of powdered, sun-scorched humus underpinned
each footstep, leaves frazzled to a fine glass.
I waded through brambles, snapping bracken,
watching bunched tails flick through hairy oat-grass,

its panicled spikelets blotched with purple,
and came on down to where a warped cow-gate
was fashioned from a sawn-up rotting elm,
the bark rimed emerald. Twitchings of slate,

or a white powderpuff tail raised to run,
showed their deployment over a warren,
rabbits turned the colour of the landscape,
textured with the indigenous pigeon-

greys and roan-squirrelings of the hillside.
They'd stop and start, overfamiliar
with their territory, but gun-shy, quick,
camouflaged soldiers engaged in a war

of distinguishing sound from its intent.
I stood stock-still and they solidified,
inquisitive, sniffing, and when I moved,
it seemed my brain-cells had electrified

a corresponding fear-centre, signals
galvanized them into a breakneck run,
eyes big, adrenalized, wanting the dark
of their burrows. Behind me a red sun

cleared the dense chestnut wood, cows leisurely
ambled a meadow. Was it weeks later,
a full moon up, I heard a rabbit shriek
on the red fuse-end of a stoat's temper?

Voles

Tail-up, quarrelsomely industrious,
two bank-voles keep poking out of ivy,
their tremulous forepaws working to roll
a snailshell to their burrow, their beady

eyes, concentrated points of energy,
their rufous bodies ticking with power-lines
of nervous current; how the needle fangs
must have bitten grey flesh housed in a mine

a starling would splinter upon a stone.
Nimble, voracious, each renewed foray
conducted with prehensile whiskerings
showed greater caution; they would move away

as if disowning their quarry and freeze
at the least tremor. Bridged from stone to stone
a spider's web was built across the stream,
a red-eyed damselfly's audible drone

was negotiating waterpepper.
My staying must have sent them underground,
survivors from the short-eared owl, the stoat,
their presence dangerous in sunlight, a bound

would have them at the throat of their brother,
the short-tailed vole, screeching in a deadlock,
the victor slinking to a pool to wash,
its heart a piston jumping from the shock.

I moved downstream, the creatures of the night
had burrowed back to cave-darkness, a crow
was shouting from an oaktop, a farm-dog
chased a rabbit ten yards, then let it go.

On Fallow Foliage

after Hölderlin

It's there already in the grape,
the premonition of the wine,
it lives there like the shadow of a gold
earring on a woman's cheek.

Marriage must be for others,
how easily the calf in slipping free
becomes entangled in its chain.

You can count on it,
how the farmhand loves to stumble
over a woman fallen asleep
knitting a stocking in the shade.

His German mouth
which lacks all euphony
disengages from a brambly beard
and moves over hers
like a stream talking rain
in patters.

The Middle of Life

after Hölderlin

Commingled in one reflection
the wild rose and the yellow pear
map out their imprint in the lake,
and swans exalted by the calm
go by with silent wakes
or dip their arching heads
into the quiet water.

When winter comes, where shall I find
the summer flowers and the sunshine,
and where the shade the earth affords?
Unspeakably I fear the walls
debarring light, speechless and cold
the wind will find me out,
the weathercocks veer crazily.

Goldfish

Piebald-pebbling,
or black on scarlet, a tiger-lily,
orange of golden-rod or apricot,
        they blow smoke-rings
across a lacquered pond and stealthily
        back from a spot

        the sun's fired red.
A damselfly fidgets on the green dish
of a water-lily, a dragonfly
        flicks a blue thread
over the square-jowled browsing of a fish
        lipping a sky

        on which willows
are inverted green parasols. Crowfoot,
water-soldier and pink water-violet
        flower in the glow
of yellow flags, a diving-beetle shoots
        down through a let

        in a surface
squiggled with the waterlights in satin.
I watch a shoal break into a whiplash,
        a spiral race
that forms an arc, they have the glint of tin
        in that jabbed flash

      back to their slow
inert suspension, little buddhas prone
to meditating on a liquid sky,
            or down below
brooding with the watersnail humped on stone,
            they come to lie

            so comatose
they seem fixtured in the ice of cold blood.
Streamlined, poker-tipped, five in formation
            flush to a rose-
smoulder, passive, never portraying mood,
            their slow-motion

            advance across
the pond freezing to an embered halt.
They paint themselves into each new surface,
            fire-strokes on moss-
green canvases, tails erasing each fault
            without a trace.

Winter Mullet

The sun's berry-red in a ruck of blue;
somewhere, recalling Webster, a robin's
melancholy song is premonitory
of blade-edged ice, frost engraining its pins

into a field corrugated by cold,
the furrow-mounts crisp as a sheet of glass.
I make my way towards a coastal drop,
the water there's nursed by a powerhouse,

a tepid current that attracts offshoots
from the densely packed, spawning winter shoals,
wedged tight like overlapping slates, silver
of a flick-knife's punched out when a fish rolls.

These are the winter mullet, somnolent,
their world shrunk to the dimensions of trance,
they are unfeeling, semi-comatose,
their vision almost dead, their slow advance

that of someone flexing inside a dream
they can't connect with. I flick a flyspoon
tipped with white ragworm out towards the shoal,
and have it flutter, a jittery moon

working the shallows like a butterfly,
invites no quick uptake. Amnesiacs,
they're living with dulled instincts, one ungroups
and eyes the spoon, but hangs there, changing tack,

his metabolic rate too slow to chase.
Two or three basking in the warm stream shift
my bait, boxers prodding at a dummy,
they lip it back and forth, hoping to lift

the worm's flicker from the barb that they've sensed.
They disengage, their curiosity's
soon extinguished. In summer, they're playful,
dribbling a dough-ball round a float, or free

to shoot ten yards at a compulsive flash.
I stay on, the cold chaps my fingers red,
its pimpling's like dried beads of black hemlock,
the fish have tightened now into a head,

a mint destined to fall foul of seine nets.
Men keep a watch on these. A figure throws
a light over me in the early dark.
I jump to meet it, moth-dazed by the glow.

Bass

My feet slide on the downpour of shingle,
the shelf rattles like a line of bare teeth
chattering in the aftermath of shock.
Rain drives in; reefs show jagged points beneath

the swell; the cold's a razor on my cheek.
The surf keeps blasting, pushing back the stones
relentlessly, and neither will concede
their tireless protestation to go on

enduring, one insoluble, and one
reducible only over aeons.
I feel the wind walk through my little weight,
my feet wedged firm I fish the beach alone,

casting beyond surf on to shelving sand,
bottoming my green crab for solitary
bass nosing in to browse with the flood tide.
Late November, big fish rapaciously

feed with the storm prior to migration,
the cold has a mackerel's glitter, a glint
of blue and silver chasing. Where I cast
the wave's out-throw is granite, quartz and flint,

pebbles scoured mint-clean in the sooty dusk.
If I could place an ear beneath the sea
I'd hear the water running; the groundswell
could finger-spin a boulder crazily;

the fish are less pronounced in murk and not
the blaze of silver in a landing-net
scooping the played out, vibrant four-pounder
whose dash was for deep water. I reset

my bait; the wind brings with it stinging rain,
my world's constricted to a shuttered lamp,
here on a beach where the sea's jaws work hard
and stagger rubble into a wet ramp.

Worm

A freight-train pulling segments of himself
out of a dark tunnel, caution not stealth

defining his momentum; the earth's weight,
pit-propped by his spiral shaft is one state,

uncantoned, primal, and without a sun.
He works the surface of its sodden tons,

a bud-pink, stringy noodle veined with red
liverish hatchings, his bore-hole's his head,

the ooze of his tunnelling the liquid
churn of Verdun. Blind, he can't lift the lid

to see particulars sharp-edged by light,
the wiry fern's tooled serratures, the bright

29

jet of the starling's flashing eyes that stab
at the least earth tremor, the blackbird's jab

precise as a knife-thrower. What filters
into that planetless black's the flicker

of a running grassblade – the thrush's foot
shifting balance, its scale upon grassroots

the tinkle of a cymbal. Dark is law
in the worm's cellarage of drinking-straw

dimensions, turning the earth with a screw's
rotating friction, cold to the cold dew

in which assassins wait. To show a tip's
to be dragged writhing from the earth and slit,

engorged and dropped, whittled down for the snatch,
a bracelet that won't shut upon its catch.

Burying Beetle

Grass ticks with the punctuated rhythm
of someone busy with embroidery –

the underpinning of a green prism,
a water-emerald, diligently

combed and recombed by the tiny bull's horns
of the beetle's orange clubbed antennae,

its restless tracking's brought to scent the torn
carcass of a vole, blood has rouged an eye

in which the terror of its death's frozen
like something trapped inside a paperweight

to be released when the membrane's broken.
Now three or four are here to shift their freight

and bury it, maggotal carrion
in which they'll lodge their eggs, they tunnel down

beneath the matted corpse, their precision's
that of a team burying a razed town

to scrutinize it all in secrecy . . .
Their commotion's a landslide to the slug's

static adhesion, the red mulberry's
a bell-buoy cone to the ant-chain which lugs

a splinter up a slope. The glossy black
of funeral cars, these work to hide the spoil

their grubs will grow fat on, burrowing back
into decay; old bones profess their toil.

Ants

Ground-level scrutiny's what each convoy
        is versed in; on the march they are
like booted soldiers hand-picked to deploy

a valley-floor, their mandibles' fork-lifts
        manoeuvring the incessant
lava of boulders and felled trees that drifts

across their path. They map a region by
        their purposeful dexterity,
so low down that they never know the sky's

more than a puddled mirror they look in.
        Vehicular, quarrying loads,
their chain-gang tenacity is a thin

red fuse that flickers like a second-hand
        wavering between numerals.
They're earthquake victims dusted by white sand,

jockeying baggage from the seismic flaws
        of a city gone underground,
firemen able to ascend vertical

faces with a stunt-car's lurching motion.
        They simmer noiselessly across
a cragged flagstone in tank-drill or cushion

a dead beetle on a mobile rickshaw,
        their bodies square like elephants
beneath the victim's weight. Fast, quizzical,

their reconnaissance combs a territory
    and strips it of each utensil
serviceable to their massed colony,

autocrats of a starved third world. Close up
    their eyes are headlights, the thorax
wing-polished by a chauffeur, their stirrup-

roll affords high suspension. Grave-robbers,
    they swarm to an uncapped jam-jar,
and sugar-drunk, mark time in the larder.

Daddylonglegs

Stood vertical the body's a study
    for the anorexic thin-line
of a drawing by Giacometti,

the legs have a spider's retractable
    pyramidal apices when
squatting disoriented on a table,

its brittleness gone slack, the plump hump-back
    resembling an oxygen tank
grounded for fuelling. Gone dormant it lacks

knowledge of the closed, room-square dimensions
    the human's ill adjusted to.
Its quirky Wright brothers' aviation

leads to a frenetic arc. Dazed by light,
    its planet suddenly too close,
this one come in out of the autumn night

orbits a humming cone of gold that burns
    each renewed enmaddened assault
on its fixed station. Nightly it returns,

its wingspan fragile as a sycamore's
    green-winged halves of autumn fruiting.
Tonight its buckled stilts drag on the floor,

it can't levitate and its whirring runs
    crinkle like tissue-paper touched
by flame. It is the victim of a sun

that responds to a switch. I can't repair
    its intricate, vital damage.
It crackles like a comb run through live hair.

Drought

The cuneiform imprint of birds' feet dry
to dust scratched ensigns that the squatting fly

trembles in; its coal-black and royal-blue sheen,
a nervous ink-stain travelling between

the light and shade, pursues a figure eight,
and drops, a jutting nailhead in a gate,

sunning, then bulleting its martial drone
into a dried-up watercourse where stones

are snailshell patterned, and the stream's thorax
muffled with leaves. Its bed is a stone track

of unrolled freightage, unkempt as a coot's-
nest shored from whatever has lost its roots,

and forms a makeshift salvage. On the slope,
a sloe-eyed carthorse frisks a plaited rope

at the squalling cloud of darting horseflies,
their tiny iridescent lime-green eyes

sparkle like planets that have shrunk to beads.
Dust is the film that's paralysed the reeds,

and given the hillside a lion's coat,
an alligator's lentor. My glass throat

pumps with the rough farm cider's stinging tang.
I lie back hearing my pulse beat the clang

of a bucket on a wellshaft, and jump
up, head-down beneath a dry water-pump.

Blackberrying

The foxglove inclines by the blackberry –
a globe on which each country is embossed,
the craters are drought straits, dust-filled quarries

my eye works into, feeling the pressure
of mauve ripeness between finger and thumb.
I turn it up for inspection, unsure

of red and green pimplings, and watch a ray
of light distilled through Lombardy poplars
silver the peach sheen of the autumn day.

Here just last week a scarlet admiral
flickered like a black pansy on the fruit,
its delicate wings too ephemeral

to outlive the month. Now my fingers trace
design and symmetry of fruition;
the light's a goldsmith tooling in this place,

where sherry-coloured leaves quiver, a flick
and they rejoin the earth, a slow moulting
before the winds impose a flurried tick

of crisp drifts exposing galled undersides.
I listen on the outskirts of a wood,
the stillness is unnerving, magpies hide

in the elm tops and chatter as I mould
a berry to my finger, and the light
spins on my outspread hand a web of gold.

Red Geraniums

Pillarbox-red, blood-red, geraniums
flourished in dusty soil, garden beacons,
all head like a Scotch pine, and inclining
to a giraffe's bent-necked posture, these won

my trust as semaphores in the dry days
when even the marching ant turned khaki,
and the green bus's visigoth armour
battered through lanes with overhanging trees

to deposit me at the nearest farm . . .
Dog-days, two shirts a day, and alcohol
inducing instant sleep. Caught in mid-word
I'd startle with a parachutist's roll

to find the clock had jumped an hour, the heat
lit spitting cinders in the head, I'd watch
clouds burn off to vapour as they came in,
the countryside would blaze at a flipped match,

the gold bracken whipped to a tiger's skin . . .
Blue-headed, red-bodied, a hunting wasp
kept hovering by a hole in the wall,
the crackle of its flight, touchpaper-crisp,

its concave abdomen armour-plated,
one of the chrysids hungering to kill.
At intervals I'd hear the constrained roar
of a bull, tethered, fenced in on a hill

it would by weight of force have uprooted
and dragged into a landslide. Sometimes I,
camping in the huge brick ramshackle house,
would find myself flinching from the blue sky,

retreating deeper, dreaming of cellars,
of watershrews, of the fox's sunk hole,
the badger's tunnelled lair, the earth diggings
of the blind-eyed, snouting, nocturnal mole.

Violets

Their secrecy of place is matched by my
adjured concealment of that spot. Each year
I come back to it in the peach-red dawn,
the wood exhaling scents of after rain –
a dog's coat drying by a fire or stable air
warm with the bull. Almost I hesitate
to reach the green moss bedded round the roots
of ageing elms, and bend down to enquire
with tentative fingers of the mauve flower
shrinking beneath the arrow of its leaf,
a fragile concentration only shared
by those who seek it out, hermetic one,
its white spur opening to meet the shower.

Moors

Are unpredictable; the scraggy pelt
of an old farm dog gone grey in the jowls
with thistles, simpering from the raw belt

the wind drives, grudging in their sparse seasons –
heather will purple, and bushed gorse ignite
and baroque chasings of fern and bracken

turn rust-brittle in autumn, squirrel-red
interleaved with gold serrations. Their farms
are rooted in wind-breaks under a lead

sky smoking with rain, a chalk-dust of wet
that blows more persistently than the air
over the earth's face immovably set

in granite foundations. Out here the wind's
a fist squeezing man and bird back by force
of indentation, turning a crow round

in the daze of its skull, swinging a chain
that's worked off cliff-faced Atlantic breakers,
torrential in their seething. Wall and lane

are the only inroads into this range
that comes and goes with mist, a stubble mat
for elements that dynamically change

with the sea's turning. Up there man and space
are in true proportion, everything vast
and flying above a riveted face,

eyes polarized to take the whole scene in,
and reduce it to the grey of a pool
his mind can magnetize upon a pin,

and retain as a crystal light pours through,
but is scruffed up, mad-cap and blown downhill,
head over heels and panting at the view.

Horse Chestnuts

The wood was steaming with high summer rain;
grape-white, the light was filtered through the trees
so densely massed it seemed we stood beneath
a green cupola, so imperviously

interleaved, that the rain was gravel whipped
against a tarpaulin, the shuck of peas
unshelled into a bowl. We stood it out,
hearing with each increase a running sea

slowed by a shingle gradient, and then
in the pauses the big drops shaken down.
The leaves were donkeys' ears, long-pointed tips,
descending like a fountain from the crown,

their white candelabra flowers extinguished
with the month. The wood smelt of hop-sacks flushed
out of a barn, and airing in a yard.
We waited, anticipating the hushed

intervals between showers, caught up now
in the rain's drum-stick tapping, each crystal
a kitten advancing on cellophane.
Was it months later we returned, the fall

of green thorny-oyster pods, split open
to reveal polished nuts littering the ground,
spiny, the green of weed on wharf jetties?
What we had returned for was what we found,

a quality of underwater light,
this time diffused with amber and yellow,
a white sun pouring through interstices,
glinting, luminous, like a vein that flows

perennially through those branches, a light
that would map out the tree's shorn skeleton
in barest winter, and give to its shape
the hard, glazed dignity it would put on.

Baudelaire's Paris

General Cavaignac stands, his swan-white gloves
defiled by a single rose-thorn of blood.
He holds the stained one like a lint dressing
torn from a peasant choking in the mud

in the morass of Faubourg Saint-Antoine –
the bourgeoisie cleaned like a herring shoal,
my step-father surviving the pogrom,
his turkey paunch braided in its martial

arrogance, flushing out the mob the way
a pheasant's beaten from its hiding place.
An alligator choking on a corpse
is more edifying than his mauve face

spitting out the gristle of the masses . . .
The days of my revolutionary youth
cool like fuming lead ladled in a mould.
Now I sniff out the subtleties of truth

in every heightened sensory response;
the muse is a black angel or the white
phosphorescence of a travelling star.
I wander through the old Paris at night,

retracing paths I took with my mother,
those melancholy walks beside the Seine
observing silks, bad oil paintings, bookstalls,
a plum-blue mist dispersing into rain,

the barges lit up in the violet dusk.
Paris that harboured Villon and Racine
is rubbled, the old quarters shaken down,
and in the effluent sewer-rats preen

their glossy whiskers. I can smell the gas
of a new age steam from a muddy pool;
the patronage of the King's counting-house
has vanished, and the poet's left to cool

like Ovid in exile. Everywhere mean,
officious, grey-cuffed bureaucrats withhold
the bullion stashed for a poet's fist.
Hugo alone erects a tower of gold

from novels thick as the steps to the Louvre.
I roll on duckboards; the one sharp dandy,
patched up, shabby as a provincial priest,
sipping an ulcerous rot-gut brandy

at a table near the *Folies Bergère*.
The couples pass, old whores upon their beat,
their faces white as plaster of paris,
they angle whale-fat thighs from street to street,

enticing me to follow. Already
I sense the dripping stairs, the muted lamp
casting a red pool on the counterpane
holed with tobacco burns, the bedding damp,

a heaped lair where the cockroach multiplies.
Pride's like the stick that gives spine to a flower,
resolute. I concede neither to flesh
nor common taste, a camel needs no shower

to make its long trek through burning deserts.
My city, where Sainte-Beuve is domed in glass
like a stuffed toucan brought from the tropics,
and won't lift a finger to help redress

the execrations heaped upon my name.
Le poète maudit, balanced on a mound
yellowed by corpses, I can feel my luck
desert me, and take off like a greyhound.

The Irretrievable: Baudelaire

My heart's a cracked bell, I can trace its flaw
through seismic fissures: it harbours a snake
engorged on rabbits, birds, its dormant coil
electrified at each jolting earthquake

that rocks me like a skiff spun round and round
on a compass needle before it dips
into a vortex. I'm always outside
the engagement of my senses, life slips

corrosively through my inert channels
and silts my veins but I can't make it start.
Those long nights in Mauritius, I was free
to touch life's spinal chord not stand apart.

I still remember black thighs, and a fire
around which men danced shrieking, lifted high,
when the spirits came down to savage them.
The stars were diamond chips in a mauve sky,

so near I counted them; my welts still bled
from that rum-tempered sailor's whistling cat
that lashed me for my priggish arrogance,
I, the young dandy with his books and hat

and disinclination to know the sea.
I festered for days in the blinding heat
of my cabin, bored by the ocean's blue
spaces, and sudden squalls that rose to beat

us mastless round the Cape. The sailors clung
like ruminative spiders to the shrouds
and spindled back and forth at the sea's pitch,
for days we ran beneath an iron cloud,

and press-ganged into service I spat out
my venom, madly cranking a pump hoarse,
my head a fragile shell in which the wind
seemed trapped deliriously. My mouth grew coarse

as any sailor, but I wore white gloves
to protect the pristine gloss of my hands,
and waterproofed my books and opium stash.
I dreamt we'd founder on Circe's island,

and greet her troop of sailors on all fours,
hirsute, pig-snouted, snuffling for the cure,
to be converted back to human flesh.
Their legs and genitals chapped with heat sores,

their queen ripening in a silk leotard,
her thighs tattooed with cerulean peacocks,
a zodiac woven into her hair.
But what we sighted were only bald rocks,

snag-toothed, anfractuous in rings of swell
that boiled to a tempestuous Alp of spray.
I longed for cafés, whores, the Paris fog
smoking round barracks, or a calm blue bay

in which to swing in my hammock and dream
of the greater riches I'd left behind
in the Byzantine trappings of my den.
Voyaging disappoints us, it's the mind

that travels through the blizzard of the stars,
while we the victims of infernal dice
need strong stimulants to appease the flesh.
We're fastened to a trundling ball of vice

by a girl's slender ankle-chain. But now
it's land we sight, or the familiar
sea-sick mirage of those who've lost their feet.
Our ship slips like a panther through zoo bars.

Baudelaire's Abyss

Our brains are crucibles of Dante's hell,
we smell the leaking gas of our own death
like cabbage rotting in a sodden field,
its arsenic coats our blood, our camel's breath

filters from flues in which our brain-cells burn,
our souls cinder to Carthaginian pyres,
and yet we agitate those flames, liquor
and drugs and venery force-feed the fire

until we hiss with autocombustion
and ignite like a torch dowsed in petrol,
a red-hot poker rammed up Lesbia's bum . . .
We drizzle through life, prisoners on parole,

feeling in everything a mustiness,
each handhold's so impermanent we slip
from a trapezist's dizzy heights to that
cavernous hold in a becalmed slave ship

bound for Morocco with its freight of bilge,
in which we remorselessly gag for air.
The age has made the soul extinct, it hangs
bat-like in a zoo-aviary and stares

at fruit placed for its peculiar sickness,
it's like the last dodo in a tureen,
men eat rather than keep God's legacy.
Chemicals frazzle every square of green

that survives the new Paris. Block on block
aspires toward some terminal nightmare
of wards for the tubercular, or cells
in which the mentally ill sit and stare

at an uncut rigormortis of cards . . .
Our journey through the city's labyrinth
leaves us confused, drug-doped and envious
of the stability of those on plinths –

old generals weathering to permanence
in bronze or stone, while we stand nervously
on the edge of the void, birds with clipped wings
denied that turquoise rift where sky and sea

are indivisible. We're like insects,
and don't dare lift our eyes to shoals of space
resounding with their silent emptiness,
and when we look into a neighbour's face

for signs of comfort we encounter sties,
an ego encrusted with barnacles
of self-love, spidercrab-brittle, weedy
as though fished out of the black marsh of hell

to pump a red pulse in our diaphragms.
And you, Jeanne Duval, hennaing the grey
mop-haired straggles of your early decline,
left the void open when you lurched away,

your head fissured, a bottle in your hand,
wheezing through salons to a workhouse bed,
coughing a blood trail on the boulevard,
the blotches resembling a mulberry's red

unburdening of ripe fruit. What I hear
is a metronomic footstep beyond
the remotest visible star, a pulse
beating in the pit of a stellar pond

on some green archipelago of Mars.
I listen, we are frozen, minutes run
between our fingers like a waterfall.
My heart's a black swan climbing to the sun.

Baudelaire in Middle Age

Fear is a parasite whose increments
expand to a void both inside and out,
we wear its countenance like the red cross
slashed on a blighted elm crippled by drought,

and yet we're dropsical, a polyp sack
weighs like a bladder at our arid core,
its pustules file into our blood, we choke
beneath the heavy swipe of Charon's oar

and raise a blue face to the waterline.
It's glacial despite the stifling heat
that grizzles Paris to a carpenter's
pepper of sawdust. Couples in the street

sense how I peel the foreskin from their skulls
with the dexterity of a fish knife
handled by a mortician – a draughtsman's
clean edge autopsying husband and wife

on their restless stomp up La Rue Cadet
to the Casino. My frosted white hair
and holed suit pinched upon the skeleton,
my eyeballs, blown up to a lobster's stare

before the boiling cauldron fires it red,
attract averted eyes. I hear them speak
of me as a defrocked priest, a debauched
scatologist whose skin smells like a leek,

and who goes hand in pocket to Ancelle
to keep his blowfly creditors at bay.
Age is a birthmark branded by a snake's
whiplash, a pip that ripens to decay,

not with the measured metronomic tick
of the clockhand on the Chambre Correctionnelle's
pea-green wall where they ridiculed my book,
but with the electric jab of a bell

warning Nero Rome and his hair's on fire;
even one's lice atrophy and shrivel
to victims of vesicular famine,
a kind of green ooze mingles with one's smell,

and work, that groove in which we place our hand,
as in a vice, and tighten the thumbscrew,
becomes evasive, it slips like a fish
through eddies, leaving me to count the blue

moons scored upon my blotter, while the stair
creaks with some creditor's thug changing foot
with pins and needles. What can they salvage? –
no grave-robber's toothpick would find a boot

worth heeling, or a saleable work-sheet.
They sell *Les Fleurs du Mal* in the junk heaps
along the quays, its parchment paper soiled
by smutty fingers. No jackal on heat

would find kindling-sticks in the jewel-cold blaze
that packs each sensuous image with snow.
Brushed by the wing of madness, I shiver
above a spiral shaft of vertigo –

the city's tiny, it's a matchstick maze,
its citizens are chain-ants thrumming by,
each with a mule-eyed passiveness. They slow,
and drowsing I can hear the wheedling cry

of a starved cat kneading today's letter
from *Le Figaro* declining my work.
I stand up dizzy like a man lifted
off his feet by the hangman's sudden jerk.

Baudelaire's *Aesthetique*

Cobalt, manganese-blue, vermilion,
the boy experiments with curlicues
and marbled whorls of colour, then stands back
in deference to Manet's truer blue

his hand can't vitalize, nor fix a light
into, his boy's thin modelling torso
toadstool-blotched with paint, as he slips the noose
around his throat, and at a single blow

sends the pin-legged chair crashing to the floor . . .
Cut down, his face is like the hectic cheese
Manet used as a first experiment,
colouring its green mouldiness to please

the captain of a mutineering ship,
the young artist watching each sea-mood change
its blinding iridescence with the sky's
troubled shoaling, learning how to estrange

then rebraid colour with such resonance
the pictorial action is poetry.
Manet, whose beard crackles like dry bracken,
whose misanthropic lips sarcastically

deplore an age that's fixed in wet cement,
its backward look into the grove of myth,
draws on the real, a city that's endowed
with the rind of the old, and the firm pith

of a new age, its neckties, polished boots,
its drinkers lobbing bottles in the Seine,
its whores' expression of lace petticoats.
And Delacroix his equal in disdain,

eloquent in his studio oratory,
maintaining that an artist worth his brush
should have a bird's reflexes to capture
and sketch a man's form in its downward rush

out of a window to the boulevard.
They shine as luminaries in the dark,
quick to perceive man's transience, his fall
the red flash of rose petals in a park

after the violence of a summer storm;
their studios designed for work, not stage-
trappings of armour, Malayan kukris,
old Gothic ironwork, things still the rage

with the plebeian, but excised by those
who see the real beneath the artefact,
the figure whittled down to a thin stem,
its floriated branchings useless facts

for the Salon's blunt-fingered exhibits.
Delacroix, who arranges his palette,
fastidiously as a flower girl,
conceiving how each tincture will transmit

a colour catching like a parrot-fish
flashing its rainbow in a clear grotto,
works all day obsessed by a change of light
he can't capture, then slips into the flow

of street life, hungry for the sparkling dice,
or gossip from his hare-lipped maid. The real's
the current we pick up on, laying waste
the marble blocking of a head to feel

a pulse describe the body's attrition,
or colour evoke music, as Chopin
conjured from Delacroix a brilliant bird
riding the abyss to the wind's slow spin.

The Treadmill: Baudelaire

A tonsured porcupine, the poet's trussed
at the expense of fiction, Flaubert, who
ransacks a library shelf for a chapter,
working all day at swordpoint, then at two

extinguishing his lamp before the dawn
catches him sanguine, dressed in a tarboosh,
the drops of his moustache starched with coffee.
He looks like someone cut down from a noose,

his body stiffened, locked with elbow cramp,
his eyes the pink of tiny squids; his pen
a jeweller's instrument for polishing.
Not so the poet in his slummy den,

distilling to compress a hundred times
to salvage one unmarketable line.
The bourgeoisie divest us of laurels,
stoning us with invective, flushed by wine

that dilates the liver to a puffy
lamprey, left stranded, rotting on a beach . . .
Gautier and Hugo live by popular
fiction; the tritest narrative's a leech

to sentimental taste – I see them stacked
on Sainte-Beuve's desk, awaiting panegyrics,
his high forehead and batrachian face
working to extract bad-taste with chopsticks,

and prune each novel with a curate's eye.
He has a peasant's love of reticence,
a mind that thuds in a narrow furrow,
and when he praises it's for abstinence,

his plump hand clammy as a camembert.
The literati shoot like tame minnows
around a self-asphyxiating bowl,
their florid arabesques and rococo

verses have a flea's legs for scaffolding;
they die before we can locate the itch
of their ephemera, jettisoned leaves
crackling to black ash in an autumn ditch . . .

I keep the cool of a Tiberius,
inviting speculation, known to none,
irreproachably dignified, the head
of a sack-covered, boot-plastered icon

dragged once around the Field of Mars, declined
the very least of patronage. We drop
our lines into a dead incense-burner,
and listen for the whistling axe to chop

their tributaries at the roots. I fish
for editors with an unwilling bait,
preferring poverty to the mad *coup*
which smashed my book in one torrential spate

for less obscenities than Zola packs
into a chapter that survives the press.
A sickly, atrophied Normalian,
he floats above the stream like watercress,

resilient, determined to endure
the wash of his own anaemic reviews.
Already he scents the first pan of gold,
the novel multiplying to a new

civic mausoleum built tier by tier
on pulp, and flying the Republic's flag,
the idle bull-nosing forward to read
like carthorses occupied with nose-bags.

The Curved Hip: Baudelaire

Fleshed out, they terrify us; they retain
the iridescence of the dragonfly's
cerulean sheath, for less than the instant
we hold them transformed, women gone like flies

to oil their colours on the trout-stocked pool.
I see them through a glass; the indigo
of a blue-skinned nymph like the god Shiva,
turning vermilion and then the sloe-

black of an amazon with a geisha's hips
and the slim torso of a boy. My nose
still hungers for the scent of mother's clothes,
her lace, satin and fur, and the pink rose

of her trembling underthings. As a boy
I'd unstopper each perfume phial, and make
a palette of my wrists, mixing each scent
until it dried into a fragrant lake

and blazed like dry sticks crackling on a heath.
At night I saw my mother's ivory
body turn to a firefly's brilliance
of burnished jewels; fear kept my memory

forever vigilant at her keyhole,
a schoolboy reading Racine's *Bérénice*,
dreaming of couches heaped with ostrich plumes,
and mad emperors showering pearls like peas

at the enmaddened mob. All flesh eludes
the form that we would have it take, its mask
dulls like the scales on an expiring fish,
we're left stranded upon a rolling cask,

resisting the pressure of a whirlpool . . .
A sou for Jeanne Duval, half a night's board
in a bordello, she who lay captive
upon my rug, tied up in silken cord,

while I ran rubies and sapphires over
her body, teasing her until she caught
them in her lips and spat them on the floor.
I'd watch her mood change to a storm, her taut

sinews working to unleash a bush-fire,
then I'd retreat, and leave her combustion
whipcracking round the room, a smelting iron
that wouldn't cool, until each silk cushion

was lacerated by her shredding nails,
a candle jetting flame on the carpet . . .
What we begin in excess, ends in drought,
a kept woman turns from an idle pet

into a lion couched down in the grass,
waiting to hang its fury on the side
of a lame-tired zebra. For nights I'd have
to take refuge outside Paris, or hide

in hotel attics, frozen, impotent,
dreaming of a woman who'd offer all
but the meshed interlacing of her thighs.
It's the wet days of childhood I recall,

a cortège filing towards Montparnasse,
the women with their scented handkerchiefs,
quiveringly upright despite their loss,
and raindrops scoring the first yellow leaf

splashed on the rimed plaque of a family vault
entwined with white triton flowers of bindweed.
That mood seemed permanent, a compassion
beyond all reach, satisfying a need.

Going Back

They spring up like round pennywort
proliferating in the lane –
faces dragging with a carp's beard,
scaled with age, tight-lipped with disdain

that an intruder's jumped the falls
into their green provincial pool –
its feudal tench and pike still browse
on rotting algae and distill

an odour of rising tear-gas . . .
I stand and smart. These seasoned shoals
of invincibly doctrinal
Methodist preachers on atolls

are singed by their unsparing fire.
Glutted with morals, they are clams
choking on their own ingestion.
Their paunches sag with fry; they jam

the unrepentant till they break . . .
A small town, I skirt its edges,
tail-up, an alighting magpie
seeking the shelter of hedges,

nervously gone at a shadow . . .
Sanctuary's never a home town,
nettled with parochial intrigue,
its laurels, senate and gold crown

melted down in a boiling pot,
its monuments lichened with rust,
its clockhands stuck immovably.
I move upon a fragile crust,

beneath me creeper-roots ensnare
the way forward; no scythe or hoe
could lop the green weeds from this ditch;
the bailiff ploughs his own furrow,

one foot in politics, one land.
I stoop to a stream's energy,
pure, unpolluted, torrential,
its cooling points to the way free,

water that's both clear and neutral,
its only motive to advance.
I cup it in my hands and drink
fragments of sky caught in its dance.

Kleptomaniac

My eye's a magnet for my hand,
prismatically it groups the things
I need but do not understand,
silk scarves, sunglasses, perfumes, rings.

What brings me here's an obsessive
desire to appease a whirlpool
whose current quickens. I arrive
at theft before my mind can cool

the calculation of my hands.
I'm marked, but uncurtailed, someone's
always behind me when I stand
deliberating on the one

object that multiplies before
my index of adrenalin
plummets. Even outside the door
my eye keeps catching on a pin,

and I return, unsatisfied,
my topcoat pockets stashed with loot.
Whatever restraint I had tried
to impose is removed, my foot

hums on an accelerator.
There's always one whose impartial
absorption's not a customer's,
his hands don't fit the crystal ball

he toys with, his deft strategy's
to watch my moves from his blind-side,
that lizard-like dexterity
with which my fist withdraws to hide

a weight that's alien, hardly warm
from contact with my skin. Replete,
my movements are diffident, calm,
I make no arrow for the street,

but linger with the crowds, aware
arrest won't come until I leave,
when someone's vice-lock grips me where
the suede patch frays upon my sleeve . . .

Today I'm safe, I've slipped the scent,
the store detective's like a stoat,
a student squatting down has bent
a brick-sized book inside his coat.

Heirloom

Your mouse-grey 1950s obstinate
Morris Minor, would wait upon the hill,
a battered perennial amphibian,
sheeted on coastal roads, driven until

its wear seemed contemporaneous with yours,
its interior smelt of wintergreen-
embrocation, it was your reading-room,
a snail's house slanted on a height between

two oaks and a mushroom-domed mulberry.
The sea beneath was like the turquoise eye
in a peacock's feather, or wintry grey,
slammed in the hollows, while an opaque sky

had lights come on like small aquarium fish
flickering in shoals round the coast. You read
for hours there, the thrillers of your youth,
the writers still alive, their novels dead.

That car bequeathed you by a friend was your
most intimate possession. Its headlights
were an ophthalmic frog's eyes, and its brakes
defied all but a tightrope walker's slight

response of pressure; you were the master
of an eccentric mechanism none
dared disattune. Often I'd trace your car
come out of a tunnel into the sun,

late autumn sunlight, and tick round the coast,
labouring the hill to this sheltered eyrie,
where gulls hung still, then lurched at a tangent
over some object imperceptibly

thrown up by the wave. Now that car is mine,
garaged after your death, its engine mute.
I walk back to your parking-spot, the waves
climb the rock-face and vertically salute.

Regular

One of a kind who finds sanctuary here,
withdrawn, pacing your drinks, circumspectly
dressed in a graphite pinstripe, your black eyes
sunk like a hamster's were an inventory

of small particulars, a pub's archives
impressed upon your mind's engraving-plate,
so many years spent watching on a stool . . .
Aloof, unfamiliar, you'd hesitate

over your choice of drink rather than have
the barman come to know your preference
between Johnnie Walker and Haig. You held
the liquid in your glass with deference

for its gold-spot of volatility,
and added water as though refilling
a deoxygenated goldfish-globe.
The admixture clouded, a tarnished ring

gone copper from the march of verdigris;
and if the liquor's burning took you where
you saw things double or in a vortex,
you remained dispassionate, a fixed stare,

inscrutable, conceding no gesture
of approbation or contempt. No one
intruded on the stool you'd ironed out.
You faced the bar like someone who has won

the right to be recognized, but ignored,
an oxygen plant drinking all the air,
so that the others laboured breathlessly,
contracting in a ring. Grease on your hair,

bootblacked its natural grey. You were a dog
begging acceptance, swallowing your bark,
following an invisible keeper
out of the swing-doors into the pitch dark.

Cornering

A hut puddled by sunlight mellowing
to amber from its jacinth source, and you
leafing tessellations of photographs
ordered into a sequence on the blue

air-force blanket daisied with ash-droppings,
nekton, or are they sun-burst shooting-stars
blown earthwards like a planetary pollen?
That one of moths dispersing as a car

overtakes the lens, shows the driver's eye
pinned inwards, focused upon an image
which cannot be recomposed twice the same.
His snouted gesture suggests quiet rage,

he cannot steer thought round this one crystal
which proves insoluble, its blue flashlight
bubbling like a police car's stalled in traffic.
These shots are your inventory of the night,

fixtures that killed time at a lit moment,
banking it on a reel you sensitize
to a frozen condensation of speed.
It's unconscious, I say, you hypnotize

before the shutter clicks the way a cat
has paralysed the bird before it leaps,
and on the instant of fastening, unthaws
the bird's mind sealed in a premonitory sleep

in which all sound's turned off, the garden dead.
I go outside and cross a field to where
a road ribbons through scutched with pimpled treads;
the light hangs off, a dusty solar flare

catching the corn-ears in a yellow flood.
Your eye can't see me level with a gate,
concentrating on detail, unopposed,
to butt the air without a duplicate.

At Midnight

It wasn't death that brought him to the door
that night when a black-out had candles glow
in solitary farms, and on the floor
one's feet interrogated things the way
a diver does, so apprehensively
one seemed to kick on upward and away.
What I remember is his standing there,
his tongue a nervous fish inside a jar,
his eyes not looking, but pooling their stare
between his feet, a withheld urgency
transmitted through each nerve, and like a hare
he shook, too frightened yet to speak, the dark
behind him that he kept pointing into
was lit by something burning, a crashed car . . .
We summoned torches, and in heavy coats
ran out into the night and icy stars
were spotting, bright fish jumping in a lake,
and found the car turned upside down, aflame.
One pair of bloody footprints led from there,
the others pointed back the way we came.

The Meaning

Lozenges of light shimmer through the beech,
the green is vegetal, a man stoops down
examining strawberries beneath bird-nets,
last winter's pumpkin has turned soggy brown,

his cantaloups and scarlet-fleshed melons
have prospered, watered snow beneath firm rinds,
and coral-pink sweet-williams show white
centres of Tudor lace, while sweetpeas wind

their shell-pale inflorescence around sticks.
The man's disquieted, three centuries
have elapsed since the Fairfaxian oak
was counted foremost amongst Marvell's trees –

the lawn a mirror at Appleton House.
He leans back in the shade, this chosen spot
has served him well in a fraught century,
he's learnt to concentrate upon this plot,

to diffuse nerve into pure energy.
He's parked his car above the slope, its blue
metallic bodywork heats in the sun,
a wing dent's knocked its symmetry from true

to a worn hunter's trophy of chipped chrome . . .
He steadies, one hand sheltering his eyes
against a light that simmers as it falls
and stays down there around his feet; he tries

to find a meaning in the afternoon,
a permanence beyond the simple toil
of tying netted fruit trees to the wall,
the past has blood-roots in his nurtured soil,

yet work it as he must, he is detached.
It's off somewhere where light glazes a hill
that life points to connectives which aren't here.
He feels that energy by standing still,

and redirects it to a fluid shape
that's composite, man bending with the light,
following its arc. Three centuries back
blood stained this ditch from stragglers lopped in flight.

Bar Stand

Your glottal drawl, a sailor's boom,
its timbre seasoned by alcohol,
audible a pitch higher than
the crack that made that small man roll

with tears he couldn't sober.
Always you must hold the pivot
to the conversation's kilter,
forcing tongues by cap and spigot

house-rounds to defer to you,
your hands spread wide on the counter,
your stoop felling your proper height,
and not just here but in them all,

a regular when you enter
on your incessant village rounds –
Suffolk to the Essex border,
well lit in each new stamping-ground,

pinkies, whisky or tequila,
amiable and jocular
with a seaman's itinerary
lending you an oracular

note to parochial affairs.
What's a village but a Chekhov
story, or a roulette table?
All the faces must turn up,

be scrutinized and reassorted,
some in different beds, and some
scandalized, then tarred and feathered.
Each head here's a turnip man.

Always you'd assume your role,
bending low to steer the talk
into a pool you'd regulate,
they the blackboard, you the chalk,

still seeking a captive ear
two hours after closing time,
parrot-eyed and squinting now,
a self-parody, self-mime.

Home meant trusting to your instincts,
ninety on dark unpoliced roads,
startling a village coven
consorting with the woodpile toads.

Smoke on Water

A tug churns in the offing, its coot-black
buffeted boot-shape treads the swell down flat,
its chugging's audible and a seahorse
of smoke curls from the funnel. Harbour rats

keep sleekly bristling by a sewage pipe.
The water's syrup with a peacock's tail
of floating oil outbrilliancing the sky.
Inshore a man stands watching a red sail

flicker down-wind. If he has time to kill,
he wears the doubt upon his face that shows
the stress of a puzzle he can't resolve.
He looks like someone counting flakes of snow

who grows more confused with each new flurry . . .
I stand and watch him. On the South Pier side
lorries are stacked with timber, and dredgers
keep slogging out to sit squat on the tide

and detonate the seabed. The man shifts
position and suns on a packing crate,
his head hangs unsupported, and he seems
caught in the drift, not opposing the spate,

but now a part of it as ripples flow
converging in the current's arrowhead.
He blends in with the backdrop, and I see
nothing to distinguish him but the red

socks visible beneath trousers gone high.
The man's the purpose for my staying here,
I'm linked to him by some magnetic pull,
my puzzling out his confusion makes clear

my need to recognize my own, and how
a common clouding shadows the clear source
we live in, creatures trapped in a rock pool,
seeking shelter before we regain course.

The Wake's Departure

They're going home: headlights flare gold across
a farmyard, startling a grey nuzzling rat
into a straw pile; some have edged the weight
of a coffin's underside on shoulders
of suits so rarely aired they hold their crease
like a cricketer's whites. Lit by toddies,
even the moribund are jocular;
the body consigned squarely to its ditch,
the talismans divided, the estate
a widow's roof-leaking thatched usufruct.
They've placed his Sunday hat upon the gate.

A Girl in Summer

Your hair hennaed a blazing marigold
was a flickering fireball through the trees,
your girl's body pinched to a boy's torso
pronounced its shape through army dungarees,

an ornamental cartridge-belt circling
the thin hoop of your waist. No amazon
exercising a spear-arm, scorched bark-black,
sizzling by the verminous Thermodon's

steaming fetor of gnats, but someone drawn
half by the sun and half a lime tree's shade,
sunning warily, only disturbed by
the constant sorties of a squirrel's raid

on remnants of a picnic, then its bolt,
the crackle of fire running up a tree . . .
I chose a horse chestnut's dense canopy,
its green light a flickering undersea

I looked up through as a diver that's hit
bottom and seeks for contours in the haze;
the milling leaves were a teeming whirlpool.
And if I lost sight of you in the maze

my eye was led into, you resurfaced
in the foggy interior of a bar,
your eyelids the pink of the dicentra's
heart-shaped locket flower, your eyeballs stars

that flashed like raindrops on a trembling leaf,
and formed two hazel pools I fished upstream,
frightened to smash my fly impetuously
on the run's white arrow gusting to steam,

but angled obliquely, missing my cast,
placing it wide, then waiting for the catch,
while you jumped up alarmed at the ashtray's
popping hecatomb lit by a flipped match.

The Deep End

The wine I drank was pack-ice in my head,
my balance rolled on duckboards polished by
the treacherous green algae's mirror-slide . . .
I shivered as the dawn's salmon-pink sky

erupted over the bay, a scarlet
sun still obscured by slate massings, a cold
light adding herring scales to the skyline.
The torchlight picking out my steps was gold

streaking over the forbidden causeway
to the jetty's deep end. I squatted there,
my rod unpacked, spooning groundbait into
the tidal calm, mesmerized by the glare

that oiled the waters, waiting for the first
quicksilver roll of a mullet's belly
to pronounce the shoal had picked up the scent.
Danger kept me alert, my truancy

from the sleeping house, my fishing the deep
proscribed by my father's admonition –
a child who couldn't swim risking the tide's
octopus of currents, apprehension

magnified my each move to diamond-point.
Like the mullet, subterfuge was my art,
I empathized with their nervous browsing,
their liquefaction, the drum of my heart

seemed amplified to carry round the cove . . .
Always I feared a stranger at my back,
the voice reproving, the indictment harsh.
I fished the tide till it flipped on its back,

lazily receding; the jetty edge
was an anvil-face of blue scale glitter
dried to an iridescent paste. I stole
back from that secret place, my feet feathers

that hardly brushed a stair in the still house.
I'd grown adept at withholding my weight,
each footstep came down on a ball of wool,
perfect in its timing, deliberate

in its subtraction of a boy's clay-feet.
I balanced as one standing on a cliff,
warding off the deep end, surprised this time
by father waiting, spine-up, poker-stiff.

Behind the Scene

Alignment's hardest, it's the billiard's cue,
we mentally perceive, but can't effect.
Words won't come right ways up when down's their due,
approximate again, we reselect,

nose down, beating out the elusive prey
we can't transfix but narrow to a track
where it's least guarded and can't shy away.
If it doubles on us we startle back

like someone withdrawn from binoculars
who has trouble adjusting to the glare.
It doesn't pay to get familiar
with where the poem could lead, the mad stare

of the red-eyed wolf-daimon's glowering prowl's
sufficient to lead on to that black pit
where blood's a lustration to those who howl,
and shades are moths inside the cave and flit

from wall to wall. But once seen, always known,
what nags upon the thread must be retrieved,
and scrutinized beneath a lamp, alone,
uncertain if the act will be reprieved

by darker forces. Rilke thought that ten
good lines in a lifetime are all we get.
Transmitting signals over a blank page,
the poet feels the tightening trap that's set

to lock him fast, and telescopically
narrows in, distracted, a fly-swatter
beating a bull's horns, nipping scotch early,
enmaddened, whizzing his glass to shatter.

Stamping Ground

At night the sibilance of rain in wheat,
and in the pauses crickets, a strayed cow
bellowing from beneath the alder hedge,
a charged mosquito policing the window,

a book picked up three times before the dawn
redly shivered through arrow folioles
of Lombardy poplars, and the green east
took on the plumage of an oriole.

A night, a day, and what's familiar here
has to be relearnt, I see near things, far.
The signposts have been altered, cuneiform
hieroglyphics, they point towards the stars . . .

But look again, on every side a farm,
couched in the shelter of a hill, defines
its durable three centuries of granite.
The rain's given that stone a pinkish shine,

but only two are farmed, a swimming pool's
an oval turquoise cobochon in one,
a Rolls is stabled in the extant barn,
another year will see another gone . . .

Heat-haze, mistings, and now the cows deploy
across a meadow, ponderously slow,
bugged by gadflies, rooting whatever's green,
they walk with the weight of four men and tow

the dragline of a chain. I start my search
to redefine a place, a field, a hill,
the cars are red and black and blue beetles
scurrying to elude a raven's bill . . .

Up on the hill I find it, a fuzzed sea,
the surf roller-skating into the bay,
each white crest having crossed the Atlantic
with winds behind it from the U.S.A.

In and Out

Indoors, dispensable utilities,
the glint of car-keys, a bracelet of change,
papers, credentials, an identity
I've grown accustomed to, and yet I range

over the particulars of a life
with such quizzical incredulity,
I seem an intruder, a bright eye-lens
polishing facts for a biography,

he lived here once, his eccentricities . . .
Outside the purple lythrum's needle spire
ranges beside the blue globe-thistle's ball
bees electrocute to a crackling fire,

the lily's a science-fictional ear
able to record sound binaurally,
a de Graaf strain with a martagon's shape,
the fiesta-hybrid pendulously

strings stamens from its red sealing-wax throat.
I go back inside, detail here's less sharp,
my pen-nib activates the universe
I select from; a spider plays a harp

in a ceiling fissure, the gold strings hum . . .
I go from room to room preoccupied
with the diadrom pulse of poplar leaves,
and how the shifting cuckoo has replied

to its own echo all the afternoon.
Wind in the ash tree forms shadow canoes
leaved across a table by the window.
Why should all insubstantial things review

themselves in planes of light? My mind won't throw
a reflection; I know of it through words,
the endless permutations of a phrase
mapped out by the black-inked feet of a bird.

Writing a Novel

Co-ordinative pressure on the keys –
the stream of liberated ribbon runs
under the punched indentation of thought.
Each type-head is the trigger of a gun,

it fires precisely through a chafed black stream.
The plot thaws then backtracks into a blue
congelation of midwinter pack-ice.
I face the dazzle, sneaking into view

a woman bolts from a car, her white shoes
discarded as she runs across a beach,
red poppies twinkle on cerulean
when her dress lifts; she leans forward to reach

the crisp, flooding insurgence of the wave,
and stands, skirt hitched up, staring out across
the smoky-blue of the Adriatic.
The left spool halts, then inches back its loss.

Flow and counterflow, now I see the man
impatiently locked in his car, one hand
drumming persistently upon the wheel.
His dark glasses cast shadows on the sand,

he sees the world monochromatically,
vexation cuts a twist into his lip.
She's hardly visible running the wave,
outpacing the supine crawl of a ship,

the Lido's beach-parasols are pansies,
the sand's a mica-glint of ivory.
He drops a contact-lens and curses her
departure, lost from sight, now wave-struck, free

to meet the future where it coincides.
These are minor characters, a sub-plot
the ribbon maps out, a hound on the scent.
I leave her running on a string of dots . . .

The Music of Blue

If there's a colour to contemplation
then there's a music too if we could hear
beyond the word eluding us, for air
is resonant with notes that disappear
on our awakening, much as the flare
of a blue match-flame turns invisible
when held up to the sun. Mallarmé's fear

was that the blue was untranslatable,
and words were quartz crystals that wouldn't flow
but interfaced themselves. Yet blue is sheer,
demanding we brush it like the swallow
with quick wing-beats, for that altitude's clear
both in the passage out, and the return,
there is a blue above the grey below.

Gradations of cerulean engage
the eye in distinctions, for water keeps
no constant hue, and I could name fifteen
subtleties of sea-green and grey that meet
on a sea horizon, blues that are green,
and how a brilliant turquoise turns cobalt,
or becomes a sultry ultramarine

as clouds compose and recompose the sky.
There's challenge here above a shifting bay
of luminous sky-lakes; such flux demands
a music that is neither blue nor grey,
but isolates all colour in one band
of light, energy fired in a crystal,
as sunlight strikes on a lit cove of sand.

Mastery of the blue means equipoise,
if vision clarifies with depth we need
motion to create resonance, the two
maintained as dynamic antitheses
create those atmospherics of true blue
that give the poem mood, as a sad man
might walk here in rain, and colour the view.

We must forever like the sea-jade sky
be moving into a new quality
of light, intent upon a music known
in the wake of migratory swifts, and see –
their arrow strains towards a hidden sun,
composing clear notes for our memory
to reassemble when those birds have flown.

Pact

The eyes are bloodshot, stringy with the fleck
blearing the eyewhites of a flogged race-horse,
a current simmers, the pulse overshoots,
re-rounding the churned surface of a course

in which the rival is an outsider
who never shows – one gap in twenty trees
something's discernible, a billowing
of light blown back, an articulacy

of hooves hammered into clear syllables,
ordered, re-ordered, crisscrossed in black ink,
the line no sooner minted than reshaped.
The pact's remorseless, all night on the brink

of unhinged reason, I've faced a scored page,
a gypsophila of effaced birds' feet
fretting back to the tideline from margins,
each new jab questioningly incomplete;

although the furrow's clear, I know its track.
And it is always so, this need to burn
thought into that especial energy,
the scales unsilvered, powder in the urn . . .

the line set quivering, the music clear,
as suddenly the outrider's restrained,
and steers the tired hand with fluidity,
and with relief the tugging bit's contained.

Apprehension

Mist as an apprehension, standing off,
all day the drag of boulders in the cove
worked through the poem's rhythm, pebbled words
resisting a groundswell,
buoyed up by the bright fibre of a thread
anchored to an invisible margin.

In the lane, a girl with red
Cornish hair jack-knifed an ivy cluster,
the berry-mace of blackheads
tinged purple. Was it thunder
clicked like two grating stone-blocks overhead?

A sign and then another sign,
the poem involved, picking out a course
with the fidgety pincers of a crab,
its legs enmeshed in twine.

Then at midnight the window open wide,
a ship lit up and standing off the coast,
the ticking snowflake of the Lizard light
pittering on the pane, I felt the thread
strum taut, resistant, holding in the night,
its owl-eyes bright, and staring red.

After Horace: Epodes 12

Quid tibi vis

We both of us nurse a climacteric,
old courtesan you slap lubricious thighs
coaxing some elephantine paunch to screw,
cajoling me with your nepotistic
favours, your presents of watered-silk ties,
but I can smell the coot's-nest bushed beneath
each arm, the three-weeks'-old make-up that flakes
like peeling stucco from your face, the wreath
of undyed hair that constantly escapes
the carrot henna. Rivals in old age,
you mock the earthworm slackness of my cock,
yet claim I manage Inachia each night,
flattening her bedding to a surfboard . . .
May any Lesbia who scorns my sex,
whose fingers are blackberried from the dye
of Tyrian purples, remember my groin
was once the platform of a mountain tree,
and even now my semen ducts run dry,
morosely marking time in a beer-hall –
my lust will gain me fairer prey than you
chalking up lewd sophistries on the wall.

Catullus 29

freely adapted

Mamurra's in discredit; only hands
who deal on a card–table, or incite
a map to redden when their feet can't stand
from some tyrannical debauch, condone
this tycoon's burning up of British coin,
his pinching the Gaul's carcass to the bone.
Puffed up with martial braid, gold-powdered hair,
he stalks from bed to bed, his appetite
keeps his fagged body grinding half the night,
this white dove, who presents a parody
of Adonis, stands pissing out his grape,
the liquid gold he got by pillage, rape,
his inheritance blown, so too the loot
lugged from the Pontic, and gold panned from Spain.
Why maintain him? This sycophant would bribe,
screw, steal, embezzle, sell Rome to the dogs
for a night's profligacy. Here he struts,
one of a breed, in soft Parisian boots,
who scatter Rome's wealth to the wind, and cheer
to see a great city razed to its roots.

After Horace: Epodes 14

Mollis inertia

Your petty triumph, Maecenas, pivots
on knowledge of my apathy that spreads
like ivy round an old oak stump that's dead.
My unwritten epodes receive the boot
of your indignation. I drowse as one
drugged on the toxic potions of green Lethe.
I juggle fragments, there's no lightning flash
to make my kite-grounded iambics run
for home. You say Teian Anacreon
dealing out facile metres for a lyre
was also struck dumb by the frustration
that raged in him for a Samian youth.
I see that you too are scorched with a fire
such as turned Troy into a blazing rick.
I smoulder on the page, stung by desire
for my new slave and his snake-climbing trick.
His flautist's fingers play upon my prick.

Nero

Is it so terrible a thing to die? –
Exile's a termite to the intellect,
one's lines resound against an empty sky
on some craggy outpost where goats dissect
a clifftop for a mouthful. None are spared,
even the household gods have rubbled heads,
the shrine of Vesta's defiled, and thunder
rumbles its omens over every bed.
Two-headed offspring, lightning bolts, a snake
a woman gave birth to, still dribbling red,
its markings interfaced with jewels, predict
the impending whirlwind we live under,
scattering Rome's twenty-one district plots
into a smashed mosaic, in its wake
a cone of fire spins to avenge this spot.

Matricide stains his bad blood with worse blood.
Agrippina, who curled upon her couch
enticing him to take her in a flood
of youthful frenzy, only had him touch
her pythonic hips through diaphanous
veils exposing her naked to her son.
He had her butchered, Britannicus too,
last of the Claudians, a brother done
to death, his gizzards shrivelled up in flame,
the whole deranged, effete imperial zoo
looking on, Burrus with his crippled hand,
Paris squawking, the eunuch retinue;
they buried him that night, even his name
was omitted from the ribald statue.

Men fear the streets at night, the drum-skin throb
of Nero's bacchanalia. He ties
his victims up in bearskins, and the mob
assaults them, gobbing spit into their eyes.
Poppaea rules his couch but cannot stem
a lust for every perversion; he rules
by virtue of Seneca's diligence,
a man whose austere philosophic school
accrues to it more riches than the state.
I envy Suillius his penitence
and soft Balearic exile; no poet
can publish, the Emperor has preference
over Lucan, my pine-enclaved estate
is eaten up by his indifference.

Our Empire cracks like worn crocodile skin,
it is a fishnet full of holes that flaps
at frontiers; Gauls, Frisians and Parthians
slough through the army's unprotected gaps.
Only in Britain does the eagle fly,
Suetonius licked a wild barbaric ruck
of troops marshalled by women – not a head
was saved – thousands stared from the horse-churned muck,
the smoking welter of a lashed rabble,
Boudicca's skin booted the blue of lead,
and yet that country's an untamed thicket,
its forests resist our tapemeasure roads.
Today our drill's the anaemic babble
of men who sit squat as paunch-bellied toads.

The model ivory chariots on his board
are playthings like the laurel that he wears
to face his golden statue with its bored
expression. Twenty times his height, it stares
towards the ceiling's fretted ivory.
The tyrant in the Golden House who sweats
beneath the lead weights placed upon his chest
for better respiration to abet
his vocal cords. His husky voice can't range
to the empyrean and when he rests
he wears a robe embroidered with gold stars.
Rome's become an international exchange
for gladiators, charioteers, mock wars,
there's not a statue's head that doesn't change.

His eye's his mirror, not a mirror stares
from the imperial rooms, in case she shows,
the dead mother who drags him by the hair
from sleep and suffocates him by a slow
immersion in an ant-hill. Nothing quells
the raging insomnia that has him run
tilting at statues, the amphitryon
of ransacked Greek gods, naked in the sun
that finds him rocking the gold statuette
of Victory, placed by the horn of Ammon;
the Red Sea's dredged for pearls to spot his room.
Whoever marries him must thread the net
of red and purple he throws at the moon –
Octavia died, a blade in her gullet.

106

The fire that gutted Rome, fanned by a wind
that stoked the blaze to a red tidal wave,
was at his instigation. In their minds
men have already placed him in a grave
the crow struts over. Things are upside down,
gold sand for wrestlers comes in place of wheat,
naumachias demand monsters from the deep
to be salvaged by a carnival fleet,
Africa and India scoured for beasts
smashed up like firewood – the Emperor can't sleep,
so must be entertained until the sand
in the arena's troughed with blood. He feasts
on peacocks encased in goldleaf, and stands,
divine exemplar of the human beast.

Profanation of every rite decrees
an inauspicious death. Men drown their words
like stones; each week a new conspiracy's
unearthed, the plotters killed before they're heard,
their heads are packed into an apple-bin –
even Seneca's had to renounce life,
his riches the Emperor's gratuity.
In Rome it doesn't pay to be a wife
who mourns a husband for she joins his pyre:
our only common law is treachery.
Paranoid, flanked by Mazacian horsemen,
nibbling aphrodisiacs to refire
his spent member, the song-bird in his den
thinks only of night. Lust heats like a wire.

Tyrant follows tyrant on thinning ice,
and each at last plunges to the black pool
to solidify. New taxes, new vice,
supersede before the old corpse can cool.
Nero, deserted by the army, ran
to some outlying villa, unprepared
for death, dusty, his silk clothes burred with thorns,
his unskilled sword-hand trembling and his scared
eyes appealing for respite. It took two
hands to assist him with the knife, his torn
windpipe gouting blood. The mob would have flayed
him alive, trussed and pitched him in a sack
into the Tiber. Now Galba's arrayed
in purple, men wish the old tyrant back.

Height: average, rarely used to good effect,
the body pustular, pitted with sores,
the features without singular defect,
but epicene, profuse sweat in the pores.
Eyes sea-blue, dwarfed by pupils, myopic,
neck squat on a pepperpot torso,
belly already slackly protuberant,
legs spindly, hair dyed gold, the voice a slow
drawl quickly mounting to hysterical
passion, eyelids pasted with indigo.
Histrionic, his one pursuit pleasure,
facetious, inordinately jealous,
hell-bent, I itemize his faults to cure
the harsh exile of one Sosianus.

VI

January

Rain in its grapeshot volleys; in the wood
disjointed elms crash, while the flying oaks
raucously thunder with a noise of surf.
Squalls sting and flurry in a rising smoke

that has cows huddle by an alder clump,
lashed, shifting mush, beaten by the whiplash
of a downpour that curds the flat to marsh,
and flogs the cowpath to a ruddled mash

of churn, footprints widening to lily-pads.
That red tractor, a Massey Ferguson
parked under a lean-to, is two-thirds mud;
rust's gobbled it from long inattention,

the farm is leaking outhouses, fallow,
red scraggy cockerels bickering in sheds
where winter pickers crated cauliflowers.
I blow my hands from blue to a chapped red

and squeeze uphill picking a middle path
between two pouring downstreams; here a fern
still lifts a pheasant's tail in a corner,
secret, enduring, like the crows that learn

to flaggingly batter into the rain,
embattled, barrel-rolling on the slide.
I get up to the wood's crown and shelter,
the fields dead-drop to meet a flooding tide,

the squall banging in with monotony,
relentless, inshore, not a gap-toothed wall
to break the head-on levelling of wind.
The wood cracks, it's as though an iron ball

draggingly thrashed the tree-tops, shaking out
sparklings of droplets. Now I start to break
for the nearest barn, coat a weighted sack,
my nose-dive startling a crow from its stake.

Foggy Days

A cabbage-head of fog occludes
distinction between land and sea,
my hands work like aircraft batons
clearing a space through which to see

my hands and then define my feet,
two blurs on an optician's card –
a myopic with glasses off,
each word breaking up into shards

that can't be pieced together. Boats
anchored offshore stand in a calm
not punctuated by seabirds,
but the monotonal alarm

of a foghorn's low, gravel-voiced
despair: a banshee wailing
for its mate across a salt marsh.
My fingertips find a railing,

a whitewashed wall, I'm flat against
the surface I had left, turned round
a compass needle that won't spin;
a damp chill works up off the ground,

each footstep sparkles with droplets.
The air I move silvers with fry,
flickering mercurial zigzags
across the grey pond of the sky,

there's no way in and no way out,
the sky's come down to anchor on
a coastline fogged out: a white sleep
pacifies the restless ocean.

Light's uniform, a monochrome
that's come to stay; I startle at
my backtread snapping a bracken.
Distance is a window-sill, flat

and levelled to a square fish-tank
I swim inside, scuffing up clouds
from the water's opacity,
a goldfish floating in a shroud.

The clamps are on; the roof won't lift,
I browse here a philatelist
too short-sighted for watermarks:
sharp gorse-spikes needle-prick my wrist.

Neutral

Green grass growing back through a stubble field
with chequered brushstrokes, thistle and chickweed
proliferating, you can feel the change –
the filtering of tiny air-borne seeds

drifting off microcosmically, the tap-
drip in the wood's the tick of poplar leaves
descending, yellow, skate-shaped, ribbed with green.
The air smells of woodsmoke, of hay-blond sheaves,

the magpie lifting's a blue and white fan
rapidly flurrying. I stare inside
a cavernous silo; a transistor
bubbles with its platitudinous tide

of universal misexpenditures,
the East and West, the claptrap of the day,
the tiny marks that don't make history,
the chaff that's either lost or blown away

through man's unregenerate militancy . . .
I cross a field and then another field,
the sky's a grey agate, the distant sea
is the blue-grey of a woodlouse's shield

locked tight into a ball in mute defence.
My footsteps terminate before the sea,
safe, neutral ground overrun by bracken,
the wild unclaimed kestrel's territory.

Distribution

A cloud, and the dahlia's scarlet sun-core
darkens to crimson, parallels of light
striped on the turf between blue poplar trees
disappear like a bird's shadow in flight,

an empty turquoise deckchair faces out
across heathland, and where shadow translates
itself into a uniformity,
it equalizes; light thinning through slate-

blue cumulus effaces the hectic
Gauguin colours, orange and red poppies
that seem embers fanned from the explosive
dawn marigolds at Moorea, the sea

a reflective laval-red tiger-skin . . .
the blaze immobilized from dawn to dark.
Light breaks again in crescents through the trees
and finds the pink glow on the plane tree's bark,

the distribution's equal on this day,
high summer pewtering whatever's green,
touching each aspen leaf with a gold spot.
Days are like mushrooms, they grow up unseen,

ephemeral, they leave us with dust marks,
vaulting the fence in twos and threes not one,
the lizard signs the earth's crust with its tail,
the sitter tilts his chair back to the sun.

From where I stand an orange kite's afloat,
a triangular pennant played to stalk
the down-breeze, it's a fish-shape, a sting-ray,
it climbs up with the wind and starts to balk,

a mouse advancing by its nose through corn . . .
Shadow and light, they alternate all day,
a summer distributed through cloud-change
touches the magpie's blue and will not stay . . .

Momentum

The wind's an iron comb coiffing the grass,
you've notched your ear into that sibilance,
a shell's convoluted pressure of surf,
its whorls hum with the teeming distances,

blades threshed into a wiry running green –
a tornado to the cricket's alarm.
You pitch back in a rattan chair; plovers
dizzy to zebra-stripes over the barn,

their flight a moment forms a boomerang-
crescent, twenty arched into a whiplash.
Your rocking-chair is an ejector-seat,
I imagine you gone upon a flash,

a pin-dot figure projected through space,
hurtling forward like a pole-vaulter who
has gone up high into a freak air-stream,
a red tie snapping back against the blue,

the light the clear haze of a champagne glass . . .
Momentum gathers in this still-life frame,
the window is a screen transmitting how
gnats form a morris-dance over the grain

that stiffens in its partial ripening;
the scarecrow tinkers tin cans in the wind,
beating off magpies heckling as they rise.
Space floods us; placing an ear to the ground,

the pull grows stronger; you crouch forward now
straining for the horizon; a skylark's
a black butterfly at eight hundred feet,
its pointed wings lit by two orange sparks.

Shell Collection

The spiral whorl, the helix for an ear,
and each shell varnished to retain its sheen,
a serendipity's obsessive hoard,
here laid out in ivory, pink and green,

colours so richly diffused, yet subtle,
evolving from secreted pigment, might
be tintings of a water-colourist,
their coruscations arranged to highlight

each in its particular brilliance.
The thorny oysters have your pride of place,
their bramble-flower pinks and tangerines
have fragile spines, they're nebulae from space,

chrysanthemums, each spiky as a mace . . .
Close to the pelican's foot, the tritons
stripped of their encrustations would, if blown,
resemble the french-horn in its low tone,

or the deep sounding of a Baleen whale.
My eye seeks out each distinct mosaic,
the tiger cowrie, and the wall friezes
patterning cones, white hieroglyphs on black,

abstract pebblings, a desert-storm's dust haze.
I search for other rarities, the red
thumbprint-sized blotch upon the bleeding-tooth,
the cratered lunar map that's imprinted

on the volute, the double-bladed prong
on the venus comb murex, stood upright
it's a crossroads sign naming fifty towns.
I pass from shelf to shelf and focused light

accentuates what's beautiful in each.
The sea's two fields away, we hear it roar,
a thunderous flood-tide fuming between
the mixed pebbles of an Atlantic shore.

Summering

Months of desertion, and the cobwebs prink
floating trapezoids, suspension bridges
in every corner, gossamer gone slack
and slatted, threads unravelled from a ridge

that once were pegged out secure as guy-ropes . . .
I open windows and dispel the must
that's mulled in here all winter, a ferment
of rotting apples loads the air, and rust

has brightened on the sills, an ochre trail
that flakes at a finger. The plank jetty's
refurbished, paint has licked its warped struts white.
Three shades of blue, hydrangeas match a sea

that's vichy-clear, electric with mackerel.
I've come here looking for the same faces
who inhabited these sand-coves last year,
searching out the familiar places

to confirm their absence, a new beach set
has colonized the waterfront. I burn
to a chip of wood blackened by the fire,
my feet kick up cinders and when I turn

I see the cave-pitted coast disappear
in heat-haze, it's a blood-speck I follow,
and not the palpable firmness of turf,
a goat-path spiralling to a hollow

in which someone I've singled out sun-tans
upon a ledge. Or are they really there?
The map's deceptive, I have overshot
the place in its reality and stare

down at a glass pebble that seems to spin –
the afternoon's a white immobile glare,
the rock pool with its nervous cowering prawns
awaits the sea's return, its cooling air.

Hiving the Light

The sycamore leaf is a lizard's skin,
the light in falling ferments in the trees,
grape-yellow, beaten out like goldleaf, thin

as the striated gauze of a fly's wing.
You're stacking paintings, mostly sombre greens,
and where your head's in shadow a gold ring

surrounds it, making you the figurehead
embossed upon a newly minted coin.
Your black hair flickers a kingfisher thread.

A vintage, seasonal translucency
bottles our summer on the coast, the days
come clear, like mullet ruminatively

shoaled in glass shallows, browsing in suspense,
each fish distinct, but like leaves on a tree
responding to one current, stock-still, tense,

then gone as though the movement was one fish,
not twenty brittle with iridescence,
their scale-flash glinting with the startled swish

of a white horse's tail viewed through blue trees.
My focus sees things now in their own light,
each particle coloured by memory

is pollen of one flower known again
before its transformation in the hive.
We put the light to purpose, berries stain

the path, the holly's hectic fruiting glows.
I watch you move in and out of the light,
leaf shadows dart like fish across the windows.

Migration

Now is the time of migration, a mist
confirms a seasonal stillness to the air;
birds spar and dart, unable to resist

the quickening assertion of that pole
which twice yearly channels them through air-flues
over continents that might be atolls

their homing stimuli's so accurate.
The air's electric with their shrill furore;
a swallow's zigzag to a spiral gate,

to strum back to the trilling of a wire
vibrant with birds, denotes the urgency
each has acquired, crisp as the crackling fire

a bee emblazons. The season's turned gold,
the russet plumage of the equinox
is speckled chartreuse and toad-brown, a cold

drops early. Bird after bird in pre-flight
expectation's nervously triggered to go,
migrants who'll fly unveeringly by night

as well as day, caught in the powerful sweep
a lighthouse throws, or seen as silhouettes
against the lunar disc. I fish the deep

channels inshore, and apprehensively.
Conger and dogfish might begin to bark
from the oil-black. The bay's a flat ivy—

leaf darkening from an ink-tinctured sea.
Everything groups before the air flickers
with an increased, audible vibrancy,

and then they're gone, the swallows first, gone high,
their bodies kindled by such energy
their blue shapes dive like arrows through the sky.

September Cycle

So looking down all summer from the cape
at you sunbathing in metallic gold
or frost–silver, I came to know your shape
sunning on a lilo, or hunched in folds

of a beach cloak, a book upon your knee,
the light etherealizing you; the bay
a flinty blue bowl siphoned from a sea
turned moody on the change. Looking away,

your eyes perspicuously shaded by
blue glasses, sometimes I would catch your stare
and deflect it, pointing up at the sky
where like a coil unleashed the drum of air

was swallows beating seaward – energy
so volatile it passed through one like light,
and wrenched one's head to face that migratory
feathered arrow in its shrill shaft of flight.

I came to know you the way memory
selects an image as a cameo,
your profile set in turquoise, lucidly
strained against a night sky of indigo,

or lonely, standing on a small jetty,
a figure also anxious to migrate
with gusting birds. Each day, predictably,
I'd find you waiting to anticipate

the sun's breaking through at noon for an hour's
concentrated and wasp-gold heat, a tall
golfing umbrella beside you for showers
that rinsed the cape silver. The plaintive call

of oystercatchers emphasized how still
the bay had grown. I left you on the beach,
our unbroken silence growing too shrill,
your body ripe for autumn like a peach.

Late Year Fog

They're stacked above the tideline, lobster pots
wintering in the cove. The fishermen
have beached their dinghies, flipped them upside down
for rain to pummel. Now mist drops again,

obscuring the backdrop to a dead year,
its dissolute links eroded, its spark
a coal patinated in grainy ash.
The wires are down, a taxi hunts the dark,

laying out traces for a small hotel
couched in its cat's-cradle of country lanes –
the white hart on its sign jumps with the wind,
and with a clatter rights itself again.

Turned soil, high hedges, and diffused droplets
of mist silvering, now a tractor's sway
weaves lurchingly out to menace traffic,
its tailboard unlit, it at last gives way

caterpillaring down a hairfine track
to a loaf-shaped farm and its fuzz of thatch.
The dark's a thistlehead, in a call-box
cold hands flick for a number with a match,

but can't get through. The year's dying in thin
voices cabled beneath the sea, a man
coddled by bourbon speaks to someone here
from a snowed-in loft high in Manhattan,

snow-ploughs shunting the drifts to yellow waste.
The taxi's found its scent, its red brake-lights
work hard on the spiral descent to where
a country inn is half absorbed by night

and half lit up, it bears a holly wreath
interleaved with ivy and mistletoe.
Someone slams a log and its embers flush
from a blue wood-ash to an orange glow.

Painting Water

Its scent already there before
we dropped down out of an oak wood,
feet planing the slippery incline,
trailing, until breathless we stood

in a brambled divide between
two gradients alike as steep
and treed by palsied creaking elms.
For months the stream had been asleep,

we'd painted its lethargic crawl,
its drugged, passive diminuendo,
keeping a low head over stones,
it seemed to be hauling its flow

out of a deadweight in the hills,
and arrived thin, a stranded eel,
its gills pumping for oxygen.
Its nerves seemed no longer to feel

for the obstructions in its path,
it sickened khaki with the drought,
a trickle puddling to an ooze.
Now after rains it drives its rout

of sticks upon its bull–broad back,
it is a logrolling packhorse
at full gallop, frothing to brake
over stones then resume its course,

the sinews taut as violin strings,
the eddies chiffon ruching where
the current's tendrils circulate.
No longer shrinking from our stare,

it wears a snake's markings of leaves,
the torrent lashing it won't let
up now, it smashes chestnut pods
into the ferment, branches fret,

the deadwood lopped by the big gale.
Waterproofed we assimilate
each water-stroke as a brushstroke,
a thin wrist dealing out a spate,

insuperable, rushing towards
an outlet where it will grow tame,
its force siphoned off by the sea,
an angry bride losing her name.